Volcanoes

by John Calderazzo

Fascinating answers to questions like...

Why is the inside of the earth hot? (page 5)

Are volcanoes good or bad for the earth? (page 12)

Did volcanoes kill the dinosaurs? (page 13)

How fast does lava flow? (page 16)

Can animals sense when a volcano is about to erupt

Do other planets have volcanoes? (page 31)

D0967920

2

Capulin Volcano National Monument, New Mexico

1

Could a volcano erupt in my back yard?

Yes.

2

What could be done to stop it?

Nothing.

3

Nothing?

Oh, you could grab your shoes and run.

That's what a farmer in Mexico did one afternoon when a volcano suddenly popped up out of his cornfield, belching hot stones and steam.

But other than that, forget it.

4

What are the chances of this happening?

Luckily, practically zero.

More than three-quarters of the earth's surface above and below the sea has been formed by volcanic action, but the earth is four-and-a-half *billion* years old and only a handful of new volcanoes are formed during any one century.

The volcanic crater near Bandelier National Monument is sixteen miles across.

⑤ How powerful are volcanic eruptions?

The biggest ones can blow off the top of a huge mountain. They can also create gigantic craters in the earth, like the one sixteen miles across near Bandelier National Monument in New Mexico.

But eruptions vary widely. Sometimes volcanoes burp up just a wisp or two of smoke and then lie dormant again for centuries. Sometime they smolder and then explode with world-shaking force, like Vesuvius in Italy and Mount St. Helens in Washington. They eject miles-high plumes of tiny rock particles called ash, or bowling ball-sized blobs of lava called bombs. Sometimes they erupt without much explosion, in a kind of slow motion. Red-hot rivers of lava have been creeping down the slopes of Kilauea almost nonstop since 1983. Some volcanoes do all of these things.

⑥ Can you stop a volcano by dropping a bomb into it?

Nope. The incredible forces that give birth to a volcano lie beneath the earth's crust. This hard outer shell of our planet is about thirty miles thick. That much rock and hardpacked dirt is thousands of times stronger than the strongest bomb shelter ever built.

Sure, a huge bomb might shatter a smoking crater. But, like a pesky and giant weed whose roots drill deep underground, the volcano would eventually grow back.

Can you slow down or postpone a volcanic eruption?

No. But over the years people have tried to please the gods or demons they thought lived inside volcanoes and caused eruptions. Sometimes they sacrificed animals and even humans to do this. Long ago in Sumatra, Indonesia, white billy goats were thrown into smoking craters.

Ancient Hawaiians believed that a goddess named Pele lived inside Kilauea volcano. She was said to have an awful temper that was always in danger of "erupting." To keep her happy, the local people threw pigs into her lava. Today, a few Hawaiians still offer Pele coins, groceries, and pieces of jewelry. But Kilauea grumbles on, one of the world's most active volcanoes.

Just what *is* a volcano?

It's a crack or hole in the crust of the planet through which molten (*melted*) rock rises to the surface to form a mountain.

Why is a volcano called a volcano?

The word comes from the ancient Roman god Vulcan, who was thought to live inside an island mountain in the Mediterranean Sea off the coast of Italy.

Blacksmith to the Gods, he forged thunderbolts on his anvil and hammered out the armor of Hercules. Smoke thundered from his oven, sparks from his hammer shot into the sky, and the whole mountain shook. Local people named the island Vulcano.

What makes volcanoes?

Heat from deep in the red-hot earth, looking for ways to escape.

Think of a pot of boiling water covered with aluminum foil. Leave the pot on the stove long enough and steam will start to slip out under the edges of the foil. Or the steam might find a weak spot and punch through. Think of our hard-crusted planet as that pot. The magma, or molten lava, gas, and ash are like the boiling water in the pot. Fumaroles (steam holes), geysers, and volcanoes are like openings in the foil.

Why is the inside of the earth hot?

Billions of tons of pressure keep the core of our planet incredibly hot — hot enough so that rock as hard as granite stays in a tar-like, semi-liquid state.

Also, radioactive elements like uranium, thorium, and potassium give off heat.

Volcano   *Geyser*

Cinder cone

Shield volcano

Stratovolcano

12
What are volcanic plugs?

Sometimes when the relatively loose rock of volcanic cones wears away over millions of years, a column of harder, solidified lava in the volcano's neck is exposed. This is called a volcanic plug or neck. You can see great ones in Monument Valley, Arizona, and at Shiprock, New Mexico.

Shiprock, New Mexico

13
Are there different types of volcanoes?

Yes, and they are often described by their shapes.

Cinder cones are usually short with steep slopes — something like ice cream cones turned upside down. They are formed by explosive eruptions of pumice, ash, and other debris that come raining down.

Shield volcanoes are wide and somewhat flat, like overturned saucers or circular shields. They are formed by successive flows of runny lava, usually over a long period of time.

Stratovolcanoes often resemble "regular," non-volcanic mountains, at least from a distance. They are formed by a series of eruptions — some with mostly lava, some with mostly ash.

14
What's the most dangerous thing about a volcano?

You usually can't predict exactly when, if, or *how* it will erupt. Will lava shoot up from a crack in a great glowing-red curtain, or just burble slowly along like pancake batter? Will the top of the mountain explode? If so, will waves of heat and poisonous gases race down its slopes? Will a tidal wave of mud from the mountain swallow everything in its path? Will storms of ash bury everything around like a dark blizzard?

What happened at Mount St. Helens?

On the morning of May 18, 1980, the most famous eruption in United States history blew off the top twelve hundred feet of Mount St. Helens in Washington state. Millions of tons of rock and boulders were blown to bits.

The glowing cloud of heat and gases that shot out from the explosion was five hundred degrees. Screaming along at 670 miles per hour, the cloud burned the paint off a car several miles away and flung it across a road. Even more amazing, the cloud ripped away or flattened every tree for ten to fifteen miles around and turned hillsides of thick green forest into gray moonscapes. From the air, the stripped and mashed-down trees — some of them as wide as a door — looked like millions of charred toothpicks. The eruption had the force of four million tons of dynamite.

Until then, Mount St. Helens had been dormant for 123 years. Scientists think it has a fifty-fifty chance of erupting again within twenty years.

Mount St. Helens, Washington, May 18, 1980

Has anybody watched the birth of a volcano?

Yes. One afternoon in 1943, the owner of a cornfield in Parícutin, Mexico, felt the earth start to tremble. The shaking seemed to come from a harmless-looking hole that had existed for years in the flat field.

Two weeks later, the hole began to hiss and throw out sparks. Then came red-hot rocks and smoke. Nearby pine trees soon caught fire. The fireworks went on all night, and by morning the volcano was belching and roaring like a locomotive — a sound you could hear two hundred miles away! Hot stones had piled up around the hole and formed a cinder cone thirty feet tall. By mid-day the cone was as high as a fifteen-story building.

Soon, lava squirted out from the base of the cone and oozed toward two villages less than five miles away. After a week, the mountain was five hundred feet tall. Eventually it grew more than twice that high, and the lava swallowed both towns. Only the steeple of a church stood above the steaming flow. The villagers had fled earlier, unharmed.

Which volcano formed most recently?

On land: Parícutin, Mexico, February 20, 1943. After nine years of rumbling, it suddenly grew quiet. Since then, it hasn't made a peep.

At sea: Surtesy, near the coast of Iceland. In 1963, it boiled up out of an ocean depth of four hundred feet. After a few months, the world's newest island was several hundred feet tall and a mile long. Lava streamed down its slopes like giant, glowing orange snakes. In places, the icy north Atlantic turned warm enough for some Icelanders to swim in it for the first time.

Where are volcanoes most likely to pop up?

At the colliding edges of continental plates. Plates are continent-sized sections of the earth's crust that push and pull against each other like pieces of a jigsaw puzzle that don't quite fit together. For example, the plate that North America sits on is crashing into the Pacific Ocean plate at a rate of three of four inches a year. (At this rate, California will crunch into Asia in about two hundred million years.) When plates push together, one plate typically slides under the other, eventually causing magma to form. The newly formed molten rock then squeezes up through cracks to erupt and form volcanoes.

Volcanoes also grow where plates pull apart, such as in the North Atlantic ocean. Except for the volcanoes that have created the islands of Iceland, these are mostly hidden underwater. One major exception is the Hawaiian Islands, which sit in the center of a plate. They lie over a "hot spot" — a weak point where magma has burned through the earth's crust.

• volcanoes　━━ *continental plate boundaries*

Which continent has the most active volcanoes?

Asia, especially in a line that goes roughly from Indonesia north through the Philippines, Japan, the Kuril Islands, and the Pacific side of the Kamchatka peninsula.

23

Which country has the most active volcanoes?

Indonesia. Next is Japan, where about a third of its one hundred or so big volcanoes still smolder. That's a huge number for a country where 120 million people live in an area smaller than California. Next is the United States.

24

Are there volcanoes in Antarctica?

Mount Erebus sometimes smokes darkly above the South Pole's icy whiteness. More than two miles tall, it spews out tiny crystals of gold with its ash and steam. Another volcano, called Big Ben, erupted in 1960.

19

Where are volcanic eruptions *least* likely to occur?

Maybe Australia. The whole continent has had only one recorded eruption in twenty centuries.

20

How many active volcanoes are there now?

Between 500-600 worldwide on land and more beneath the sea.

21

Where are most of the active volcanoes?

Mostly along the so-called Ring of Fire. This is a roughly circular zone of volcanoes and earthquakes that wraps around the Pacific Ocean. It runs through Alaska, Canada, Washington, Oregon, California, Mexico, Central America, and the Andes. Across the Pacific it includes New Zealand, Indonesia, the Philippines, Japan, and the Kamchatka peninsula of Siberia.

What parts of the United States are most threatened by potential eruptions?

Yellowstone National Park, with twenty-five hundred geysers, fumaroles, and other geothermal hot spots, is certainly *restless*. The world's first national park lies at the meeting point of three major fault lines and each day averages five earthquake microschocks, or tiny earthquakes, that indicate geologic shifting deep underground. But there's no evidence that Yellowstone is becoming hotter.

Kilauea on the big island of Hawaii has been erupting for years, and two other volcanoes there have erupted during the last two centuries. Other good bets for major volcanic action are the Mammoth Lakes area of eastern California and Mt. Rainier, Washington.

In the continental United States, the last few hundred years have seen earthquakes in Indiana, South Carolina, and the Atlantic coast. Still, nothing volcanic has occurred in the United States east of the Rocky Mountains for millions of years.

How many volcanoes are active in the United States?

About thirty-five. This includes Mount Shasta and Lassen Peak in California; Mount Hood and Crater Lake in Oregon; Mounts Baker, Rainier, and St. Helens in Washington; and Kilauea and Mauna Loa in Hawaii. Alaska has many more, including Katmai. When Katmai erupted in 1912, so much ash poured out of its vent and fumaroles that one of its valleys was named The Valley of Ten Thousand Smokes.

Mount Shasta, California

Are all islands created by volcanoes?

No. Long Island, England, and Ireland are examples of non-volcanic islands. Island volcanoes are just volcanoes that pushed up through the earth's crust in a place that was already — or is now — covered by water.

Well-known examples are the Aleutians, the Galapagos, Hawaii, Iceland, Iwo Jima, Japan, Martinique, and Sicily.

Red-hot lava from Kilauea volcano meets the Pacific ocean, producing steam and creating new shoreline on the island of Hawaii.

How long has the earth had volcanoes?

Probably for most of its four-and-a-half billion years of existence. We humans have been walking around for only a million years or so. That's less than a *thousandth* of the time the earth has been sailing through the universe — in geologic time, the blink of an eye.

30

Are more volcanoes erupting now than ever before?

Well, more are being *reported*. We have better measuring tools, and many more people now live in remote areas. Recent years have seen some really big eruptions, like Mount St. Helens and Pinatubo in the Philippines. But volcanologists think the earth is probably "renewing" itself through volcanoes at about the rate it always did. In an average year, about twenty-five new eruptions occur worldwide.

28

Do all mountain ranges have volcanoes?

Not necessarily. Some "young" ranges such as the Himalayas and the Alps don't. Instead of being formed by volcanoes, both were pushed upward as continental plates crunched into each other over millions of years. In fact, they are still growing.

Are volcanoes good or bad for the earth?

Billions of years ago, the earth was a rock that resembled a celestial ping pong ball — with no mountains, no lakes, no rivers, and no oceans. Meanwhile, radioactive rocks inside the planet were gradually decaying and heating up.

Over millions of years, hard rock melted and oozed out where the crust was weakest, making volcanoes, lava flows, and hills of ash. The lava also released water vapor and carbon dioxide, which swirled over the globe. This water helped to fill the oceans. Along with other geologic forces, it also helped to carve valleys and mountains.

Without volcanoes, the earth wouldn't look like it does today. And we wouldn't be here to know the difference.

Can volcanoes change the weather?

Large eruptions that eject lots of fine ash into the atmosphere can temporarily cool the earth. It's thought that the veil of ash that Mount Pinatubo sent around the planet in 1991 deflected about 2 percent of the sunlight we normally receive. During the next few years, the average temperatures on earth dropped about one degree.

Why do volcanoes make red sunsets?

Let's take the Philippines; Mount Pinatubo, which in 1991 became this century's second or third biggest eruption. It left thousands homeless and wrecked a United States air force base. It also spewed sulfur gas up to sixteen miles into the atmosphere. The gas mixed with water vapor and formed drops of sulfuric acid. These tend to scatter wavelengths of sunlight, especially red and orange. Only three weeks after the eruption, a fine mist had circled the planet. This made gorgeous sunsets and sunrises — a Pinatubo Glow.

But it's not always red. In 1883, Krakatau tinged sunsets green and made the moon look blue.

Do big eruptions of ash and chemicals hurt the ozone layer?

This is an important issue because the ozone layer, a part of the atmosphere that lies 6 to 30 miles above the earth, helps to block the sun's cancer-causing rays.

Large eruptions like the Philippines' Mount Pinatubo can shoot 10-20 million tons of sulfur fifteen miles or higher into the sky. Thus, the answer is probably yes.

Can ash or smoke from a volcano escape into outer space?

No. The earth's *escape velocity* is twenty thousand miles per hour. That's the speed that something solid would have to reach to break free from the tremendous pull of gravity. Even volcanoes can't shoot anything into the sky with that speed.

What in the world is "vog"?

Volcanic smog, the kind you might see along the coast in Hawaii, where hot lava from Kilauea pours into the ocean. A mist composed of steam and hydrochloric acid sometimes gathers in places where the newest land on earth — lava — hisses into the surf.

Did volcanoes kill the dinosaurs?

The dinosaurs became extinct about sixty-five million years ago. Some scientists think meteors caused it. Others say that ash clouds from giant volcanoes on India's Deccan Plain may have circled the globe, cooled the world's weather, and killed these beasts.

What was the biggest volcanic explosion in history?

The 1815 eruption of Tambora in Indonesia. It blew off the top of its cone and left a caldera — or pit-like depression — four miles wide and half a mile deep. The gigantic ash clouds from Tambora created complete darkness for three straight days three hundred miles away!

Another big bang was Krakatau, also in Indonesia. This island-volcano's 1883 blowout created giant sea waves that wiped out more than one hundred coastal villages and killed thirty-six thousand people.

Then there was the Mediterranean island of Santorini. In 1470 B.C. it erupted violently and collapsed on itself, leaving a caldera more than six miles across. Some scholars have thought the resulting sea waves and ashfalls caused the Minoan civilization on nearby Crete to suddenly die out. People have wondered if Santorini was Atlantis, the legendary island empire that is said to have sunk under the sea in a day and a night.

What were the biggest explosions in the United States?

The ones that took place in what is our oldest national park — Yellowstone. (In fact, the park gets its name from chemically stained volcanic rock.) A Yellowstone eruption six hundred thousand years ago spewed so much ash into the sky that even two hundred miles away the tiny dark particles rained down in a layer that would bury a six-story building.

Two other giant eruptions took place more than a million years ago near what's now Bandelier National Monument, not far from Santa Fe, New Mexico. Each was more than six hundred times as explosive as Mount St. Helens. They left a hole in the ground 16 miles across and a lava field at least forty miles wide.

Mount St. Helens, Washington, July 22, 1980

How many people have been killed by volcanoes worldwide?

Over the last five hundred years, a few more than 250,000 worldwide. Among natural disasters, earthquakes, floods, and typhoons have killed far more people.

Has anybody famous died in a volcanic eruption?

While Vesuvius was erupting in A.D. 79, the Roman writer and naval officer Pliny the Elder ordered a boat to take him across the Bay of Naples for a closer look. To protect himself from the frightening storm of falling stones and cinders, he tied a pillow on top of his head. Nevertheless, Pliny died from either a heart attack or poisonous gases.

What was the single most deadly volcano?

Tambora, in Indonesia — it killed ninety thousand people in 1815. Its huge blast scooped out a crater four miles wide where the top of the volcano had been.

But the blast itself killed "only" a few thousand people. A frightening rain of ash killed the others — at least indirectly. For miles around, noon turned into midnight, and thousands of productive farms became moonscapes. Soon after, far more people died from starvation than from the eruption itself.

Volcanoes hurt a lot of people. How do they help?

Over hundreds of millions of years, volcanoes have helped give us the air and water we need to stay alive.

Volcanoes also grow into spectacular mountains and rock formations that we hike and climb on, tell stories about, or simply love to look at. Formations as different as Shiprock in New Mexico and deep blue Crater Lake in Oregon were formed by volcanoes. In some cases diamonds, gold, and other valuable minerals can be found to have formed near volcanoes.

Is volcanic soil good for growing crops?

Some of the world's best farmland lies near or on the slopes of volcanoes that erupted long ago. Italy's Mount Etna and Vesuvius support miles of rich vineyards that grow out of black volcanic soil. According to one popular theory, about one thousand years ago Arizona's Sunset Crater Volcano dropped ash and cinders over a huge area of desert. Decades later, Sinagua Indians discovered that the rich, dark soil was good for growing corn and other foods. More people than ever before moved to the Sunset Crater area.

Can we tap energy from volcanoes?

Towns in New Zealand, Italy, Iceland, California, and elsewhere derive heat or make electricity by tapping geothermal wells drilled into volcanic fields. Heat from the earth turns water to high-pressure steam, which powers turbine generators without polluting the air the way coal-fired power plants do.

There are limits to how much volcanic energy we can harness, though. We can do nothing but watch — from a safe distance — the fantastic energy released by a big eruption. The thousands of small and steady geothermal steam eruptions in Yellowstone Park give off enough heat to melt three tons of ice day. But harnessing these geysers and fumaroles would ruin them and the park.

Drilling steam wells just outside the park boundary might drop the pressure under natural wonders like Old Faithful geyser. Geothermal tapping has killed nearby natural steamholes in Nevada and New Zealand.

Aa lava from the McCarty flow, El Malpais National Monument, New Mexico

(Background: Pahoehoe lava)

How fast does lava flow?

If it's very runny and sliding down a steep slope, up to fifty miles an hour. That's more than twice as fast as the fastest human can run. Usually, though, it moves much more slowly. Thick, crunchy lava often clinks and crackles along at a walking pace or even more slowly.

Of course lava exploding from the neck — or throat — of a volcano is a different story. Millions of tons of pressure can hurl small gobs into the sky like cannon balls.

Castle geyser, Yellowstone National Park

How much lava comes out of volcanoes?

A glowing trickle or a raging river of fire — it depends on the amount of force behind the eruption and the size of the magma chamber beneath the volcano. In recent years, Kilauea has gushed enough lava to bury Los Angeles. In 1783, lava burst from Laki in Iceland and sizzled along for forty miles. There may be much bigger flows on the ocean floors, which are mostly covered with lava.

Does lava make noise when it flows?

Sometimes it crackles and crunches. A skin of "glass" can form on its surface as it cools. The glass often breaks when the lava underneath keeps moving. Escaping gases also make noise.

Can anything stop lava?

In 1669, workers from Catania, Sicily, used picks and shovels to redirect a Mount Etna lava flow heading for their town. They tried to channel it toward nearby Paterno. The people in Paterno got angry. Finally the towns made a truce: Nobody messes with the lava. Etna's tenth major eruption of this century occurred in 1992. When a thirty-foot-thick tongue of lava slid from a crack in the volcano's side and threatened the town of Zafferana, soldiers built a five-story high earthen wall to redirect the flow. The flow stopped on its own very close to the wall.

In 1973, lava crawled toward the Icelandic village of Heimay and its harbor. It lifted houses off their foundations and crushed others. The villagers fought back with giant pumps and firehoses, cooling the flow with millions of gallons of seawater. The battle took weeks, but the lava darkened, slowed, and stopped on the edge of the harbor. Did the villagers succeed? Some people think the lava was slowing down anyway.

How hot does lava get?

Often it's about two thousand degrees. That's ten times the temperature it takes to boil water. But it's only one-sixth as hot as the earth's solid iron core.

How long does lava take to cool?

A lava flow starts cooling as soon as it hits air. But deep lakes of molten lava — thick rock soup — can take up to twenty-five years to cool and turn solid.

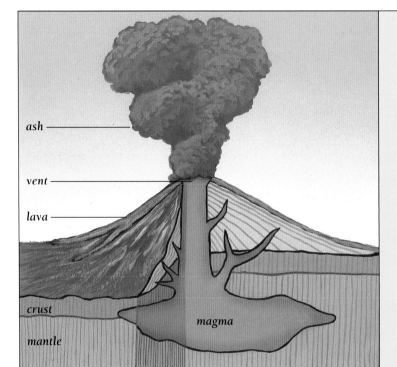

ash

vent

lava

crust

mantle

magma

What's lava made of?

The ingredients are just about the same in all types of lavas, but the proportions vary a great deal.

Easily the most common ingredient is silicon dioxide. Others include oxides of aluminum, sodium, potassium, iron, magnesium, and calcium. Depending on how much silicon dioxide is present, lavas are categorized as rhyolites, basalts, and andesites.

Pahoehoe lava

Is lava the same wherever it appears on earth?

No. Thick, slow lava that cools into a rough and jagged surface is called **aa**. It's pronounced "AH-ah," like the sound you might make if you tried walking over it barefoot even millions of years after it cooled. **Pahoehoe** (Pa-HOY-HOY) is smoother, runnier, and flows along like bright orange cake batter. Both words are Hawaiian. You can find excellent examples of both kinds of lava at Sunset Crater Volcano National Monument, near Flagstaff, Arizona.

Aa lava

What's the difference between lava and magma?

Magma is just lava before it breaks through the earth's crust and releases its gases at the vent — or opening — of the volcano.

What's a lava tube?

Because a long flow of lava always cools fastest on its outside borders, hot lava in the middle of the flow sometimes keeps sliding along after the outside walls have solidified. Sometimes this hot lava empties out, leaving a volcanic tunnel — or lava tube. You can see these at El Malpais National Monument in New Mexico and Lava Beds National Monument in California.

Entrance to Heppe cave, a lava tube at Lava Beds National Monument, California.

Does lava have household uses?

Often volcanic rocks are used in household gardens and barbecue pits. They're called common scoria — orange-brown, red, or black rocks pocked with tiny holes, like hard sponges. Outside the house, they're used in the sand traps on Hawaiian golf courses. Pumice stones are soaked in chemicals and tumbled in giant washing machines to "stone-wash" jeans and other clothes.

Ancient people in the Americas found much more practical uses for lava. They made knife and ax blades from obsidian, a natural volcanic glass. They also used basalt and andesite to grind things with.

What caused the bubbles you see in volcanic rock?

Volcanic gases and air. The more bubbles, the lighter the rock. Pumice is a kind of rock loaded with bubbles — so many that it sometimes even floats! At Capulin Volcano National Monument in northern New Mexico, you can find rocks as big as beachballs and and lift them with one hand.

Pumice

19

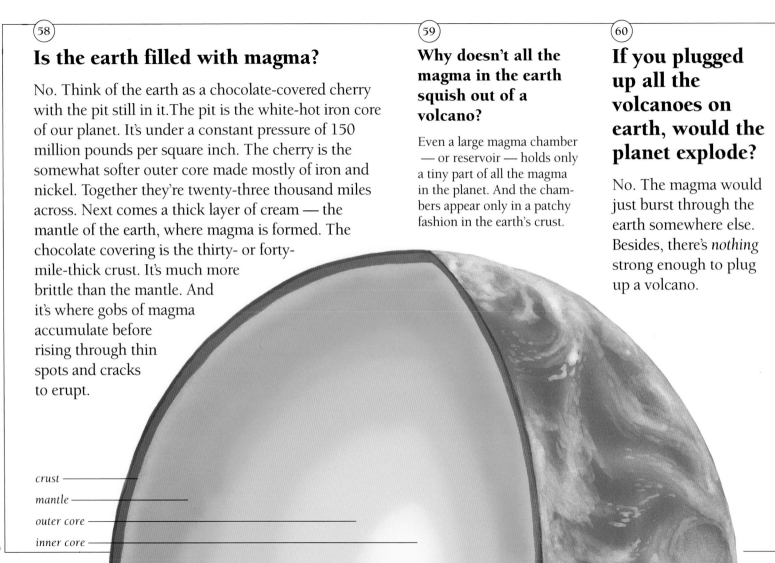

Is the earth filled with magma?

No. Think of the earth as a chocolate-covered cherry with the pit still in it. The pit is the white-hot iron core of our planet. It's under a constant pressure of 150 million pounds per square inch. The cherry is the somewhat softer outer core made mostly of iron and nickel. Together they're twenty-three thousand miles across. Next comes a thick layer of cream — the mantle of the earth, where magma is formed. The chocolate covering is the thirty- or forty-mile-thick crust. It's much more brittle than the mantle. And it's where gobs of magma accumulate before rising through thin spots and cracks to erupt.

crust

mantle

outer core

inner core

Why doesn't all the magma in the earth squish out of a volcano?

Even a large magma chamber — or reservoir — holds only a tiny part of all the magma in the planet. And the chambers appear only in a patchy fashion in the earth's crust.

If you plugged up all the volcanoes on earth, would the planet explode?

No. The magma would just burst through the earth somewhere else. Besides, there's *nothing* strong enough to plug up a volcano.

Can a "regular," non-volcanic mountain suddenly turn into a volcano and explode?

No. A brand-new volcano would have to drill its way straight up through all that rock. It's much more likely to follow a path of lesser resistance and squirt up somewhere else, where a mountain didn't already exist.

Do some volcanoes never stop erupting?

The island volcano of Stromboli, near Sicily, may come closest. For all of recorded history, it's been shooting up great orange splatters of lava every ten to fifteen minutes. If you stood on its pitch-black, volcanic rock beaches you'd hear the top of the mountain exhaling like a dragon.

How far can volcanoes throw rocks?

Pieces of ash can be as small as specks of dust and can be hurled miles into the air. Then, winds can push them almost anywhere in the world. Even heavy, basketball-sized "bombs" can be catapulted thousands of feet from the crater.

Can a volcano grow up through an oil deposit and "strike oil"?

Very unlikely. Indonesia has lots of oil and lots of volcanoes, and it's never happened there. Even if it did, we might not realize it. The tremendous heat of the magma would turn the oil to gas.

Can an oil well driller accidently break into magma and cause an instant volcano?

Almost impossible. At a depth of five or six miles, the world's deepest oil wells are easily deep enough to "strike" magma. But even the hardest drill bit would start to warp or melt by the time it got close to this boiling rock soup. However, in 1977 geologists bored holes in Iceland's Krafla volcano to tap geothermal heat. Magma found its way into one of the holes, and out poured three tons of lava!

(66)

What does a volcano smell like?

"Dead" and dormant — or long silent — ones smell like regular mountains — pine trees, wildflowers, sage, whatever. The vents and steamholes of active ones can often give off a strong smell of sulphur.

(67)

Are lava and ash radioactive?

Sure, and so are practically all the rocks in and on the earth, but at such low levels that they're harmless. Take a chunk of granite the size of a baseball. If you could gather all the radioactivity that would be released from it over the next ten million years, you could boil a cup of hot chocolate.

(68)

How can things grow again after a volcano has coated the landscape with ash and lava?

Capulin Volcano in New Mexico is green with pines, junipers, and shrubs. But after its last eruption ten thousand years ago, only dark cinders and acres of lava covered this spectacular cinder cone. Over the years, the wind blew dust and small seeds onto its cooling slopes, to be caught by the heavily pocked volcanic rocks. The dust made tiny gardens for these seeds and others that were brought by birds and animals. The gardens made good homes for seeds of bushes and trees. As they grew, their spreading roots held even more new soil to the once-bare slopes. The roots also helped to break down the pieces of lava.

On some volcanoes tiny plants and grasses may start growing back within months. (At Mount St. Helens, pocket gophers that survived the blast by staying underground quickly brought rich soil to the surface as they burrowed for roots and bulbs.) A thick forest may take decades or centuries to return, depending on rainfall.

Kilauea Iki lava lake, Hawaii Volcanoes National Park, Hawaii

22

How does lava get up over the edge of a very deep crater?

Sometimes it just piles up and flows over like cake batter. Other times, though, the sheer weight of the lava in the crater may force the magma below it to wriggle an easier path to the surface. It may squeeze out the side of the volcano or pop up somewhere else. And sometimes lava bombs shoot high into the air like rocks from a catapult.

Can you take a million-year-old chunk of volcanic rock and melt it back into lava?

Sure, if you have the right equipment. In a strong pressure chamber, a chunk of basalt will start to soften at about twelve hundred degrees. At two thousand degrees it's ready to flow.

Can we predict when a volcano will erupt?

In 1977, volcanologists on the Caribbean island of Guadeloupe expected Soufriere volcano to explode and moved 70,000 people from their homes and businesses. Everyone waited — often angrily — for three months. Nothing happened.

Scientists have done better elsewhere, and especially more recently. The eruption of Pinatubo in the Philippines in 1991 was accurately predicted and people were evacuated. But success depends partly on being able to set up some very sensitive equipment in or near craters. The instruments measure tiny earthquakes, the release of gases, and even bulges as small as a quarter of an inch in the volcano itself. The faster these things increase, the sooner the volcano is likely to erupt. Predictions at a few well-studied volcanoes are now much better.

We still need to improve, especially because worldwide about one in ten people lives close to a volcano. For example, two million people in Naples, Italy, live on or near the slopes of Vesuvius.

If you're on a volcano and it gets very windy, does that mean it's about to explode?

Rangers in some of our volcanic national parks and monuments hear this question a lot. The answer is no.

The only "weather" that genuinely affects volcanoes is the subterranean kind — the shifting and grinding of continental plates.

Do volcanoes have "favorite" times of the year to erupt?

No. The molten rocks and gases that simmer miles below us don't care whether roses are blooming or snow is falling.

Do the positions of the moon, planets, and stars affect volcanoes?

Astrologers and other fortune tellers might say so, but *astronomers*, volcanologists, and other reputable scientists probably wouldn't. (Horoscope for a volcano: "You're in for a bad day. Try not to blow your top.")

Of course, the moon really does pull ocean tides. It even slightly bends the earth's crust, which is six times more rigid than steel.

Over the years, volcanologists have wondered if a volcano can be triggered by tides or sun spots — gigantic gas explosions on the surface of the sun. We know that sunspots occur in eleven-year cycles and affect radio waves and maybe our weather. But volcanoes? Doubtful.

Do earthquakes happen every time a volcano erupts?

Yes, though the earthquakes don't usually continue after the eruption starts. But sometimes they're so small that nobody notices. And other times they're big — the earth readjusting itself to the shifting pressures of magma. Mount Pinatubo experienced four hundred earthquakes in two days before it erupted.

Can animals sense when a volcano is about to erupt?

Maybe. There have been a few such stories. Deer and other animals have an amazing sense of smell. This might help them notice tiny gas leaks from cracks in the earth near a volcano or small changes in geysers or fumaroles. Volcanoes often give off more gas before they erupt. Animals can also sense sounds and vibrations that humans can't. Still, animals do get caught in eruptions.

How can you tell if a volcano is really dead?

The longer a volcano is silent, the better the odds it will stay that way. But some have thundered back to life fifty thousand and even a million years after becoming "extinct." That's a word that volcanologists no longer like to use.

Vesuvius in Italy and Tambora in Indonesia were thought to be long dead when they went off, killing thousands. Legend tells us that cats have nine lives. History proves that volcanoes can have hundreds.

How dangerous is it to study volcanoes?

Lava bombs, ash storms, poison fumes, jets of steam, high and crumbling mountains — the scenery's great, but job conditions for volcanologists can be tough. Scientists try to protect themselves with gas masks, heat-resistant suits, and careful planning. Most lead far *less* dangerous lives than policemen or firemen.

Volcanoes are treacherous, though. A French couple named Maurice and Katia Krafft were the leading volcano photographers in the world. They climbed more than half the globe's active volcanoes and once even paddled a rubber raft on an African lake full of sulfuric acid. But in 1991, on Japan's Mount Unzen, they were killed in an explosion of heat and gas. More recently, half a dozen volcanologists were killed by an unexpected eruption while they were inside the crater in a Columbian volcano.

How far away should you go to be safe from an eruption?

With protective clothing and the expert guidance of volcanologists, researchers can easily toast marshmallows over lava flows in Hawaii — as long as the lava crackles along slowly and steadily, that is.

Yet from a distance of hundreds of miles, the biggest ashfalls can blanket the landscape and make breathing difficult.

What do we *not* know about volcanoes?

Lots! How does magma move? From how far down does it rise? How quickly? Exactly when will a smoking volcano finally erupt?

Scientists are just starting to "map" magma reservoirs — the pockets of magma that lie beneath volcanoes. They do this by shooting sound waves about twenty-five miles into the earth's crust and seeing what they bounce off of.

But this new leap in technology is really just scratching the surface of the planet. If the thirty-six hundred-mile distance from your backyard to the very center of the earth were represented by a football field, these new probes would go only as far as the two-yard line.

Kilauea volcano, Hawaii Volcanoes National Park, Hawaii

What would happen if you jumped into an active volcano?

It would be the last volcano you ever saw. And believe it or not, some people have done this *voluntarily*.

The Greek philosopher and poet Empedocles (em-PED-do-klees) flung himself into Mount Etna in Sicily. He was supposedly trying to show his followers that he was a god. That's the last anyone heard from him.

In ancient Japan, as many as one hundred people a year threw themselves into craters to become closer to gods.

If you flew an aircraft over an exploding volcano, would you crash?

If you were close enough, and if the blast produced a lot of ash, you might. Even well after the eruption, the thick clouds of ash could clog jet engines miles away. In 1983, a Boeing 747 flying at a height of forty thousand feet between Malaysia and Australia had all four of its engines stall when it flew through the ash of a nearby eruption. The plane dropped almost five miles before the crew managed to restart three of the engines.

Lava fountain eruptions are less dangerous to aircraft, and scientists have used helicopters to observe and monitor them at close range.

What would happen if a volcano erupted under a glacier or other thick ice?

You'd see lots of steam as the ice melted. Lava might cool and slow down quickly — at least until the volcano broke through the ice. Tremendous floods could occur, as they have in Iceland. Or giant mudflows could smother everything in their path.

84

How can there be glaciers and snow on active volcanoes?

A smoking volcano is warm on the surface only around the vent and maybe near some fumaroles. These are holes in the ground — often just 10-20 feet wide — that give off steam or hot gases. The red-hot magma rising through the middle of the mountain has too much rock and soil between it and the slopes to melt any snow.

Mt. Rainier National Park, Washington

85

What's the difference between volcanoes born at sea and those on land?

Either way, magma breaks through the earth's crust and turns to gas, lava, and ash.

When the bottom of the ocean first cracks open, little or no ash or smoke reaches the surface. But in shallow seas, steam may escape through giant black bubbles that break on the surface.

Lava squirting up through the sea floor looks like popcorn exploding in slow motion — bright orange and red blobs almost instantly darkening as they cool.

86

Why doesn't ocean water pour into an underwater volcano and "snuff it out"?

The lava and gases squeezing from a volcanic vent in even the deepest seas exert greater force than the water.

What's the tallest volcano on land?

Aconcagua, Argentina. 22,831 feet. It's also the tallest mountain in the western hemisphere. Dormant.

What's the tallest volcano at sea?

Mauna Kea, Hawaii. 33,000 feet. That's right, it's about 4,000 feet taller than Mount Everest and more than six miles from top to bottom, which makes it the tallest volcano on the earth. Only the top 13,800 feet of what Hawaiians call "Snow-covered Mountain" is above the water. Its base on the ocean floor is seventy miles wide.

Mount Everest (non-volcanic) 29,000 feet

Aconcagua 22,831 feet

Mauna Kea 33,000 feet

sea level

vertical scale exaggerated 10 times

What was the loudest volcano?

The Indonesian island-volcano of Krakatau erupted in 1883 with a force equal to three thousand atomic bombs of the size dropped on Hiroshima, Japan, during World War II. The blast was so loud you'd have thought the earth itself was shouting into space. It cracked windows one hundred miles away and was heard by a coast guard observer *three thousand miles to the west*. He said it sounded like the roar of distant guns. If a mountain in Colorado exploded with the same force, everyone in the United States would hear it.

Are there "silent" volcanoes?

In a way, yes. These are the hot tongues of magma that are still working their way up through the earth's crust, like branches of a tree. They may seem quiet now, but sooner or later we'll certainly be hearing from them.

Can volcanoes cause tidal waves?

Yes. The eruption of Krakatau created *tsunamis* — tidal waves caused by underwater earthquakes or volcanic eruptions. Some rose to the height of a six-story building and raced across the ocean at three hundred miles per hour. These terrifying walls of water caused most of the Krakatau's thirty-six thousand deaths. The next day a much smaller tsunami was noticed in the English Channel, halfway around the world.

What are some famous volcano legends?

The Roman poet Virgil wrote that, when Emperor Julius Caesar died in 44 B.C., the sun felt sorry for the Roman Empire and covered its beaming face with darkness. We know now that a huge volcano exploded that year and its ash dimmed the sun.

In Japan, the grandson of the sun-goddess once set foot on top of Takachiho volcano. From this meeting of sky and earth came the long line of emperors. From them came the Japanese people.

How did people long ago explain volcanoes?

Often they worshipped or feared their fire mountains as the homes of gods or demons. Some early Christians thought of smoking craters as the gateways to hell and their endless rumbling the shrieks and groans of departed sinners.

But in Japan, the volcano Fujiyama has long been a symbol of eternal life. Over the centuries, thousands of pilgrims have climbed its gracefully curving slopes.

The Greek philosopher Plato in 400 B.C. thought the earth was a globe with a river of fire running through its center, and that the fire escaped through volcanoes. His concept proved to be remarkably accurate.

A Chehalis Indian legend says that Mount Rainier and Mount St. Helens — both thought to be females — had a fight over the male Mount Adams. The women threw hot rocks and fire at each other until Rainier was hit so hard that her head broke off. This probably referred to an old eruption. All three mountains, in what is now the state of Washington, are volcanic.

According to a Cheyenne legend, seven brothers sought to escape from a grizzly bear by climbing up a huge stone tower. They prayed for the tower to lift them above the bear's reach. As they rose into the sky, the bear's sharp claws left long scratches in the rock. This is Wyoming's Devil's Tower, one of the most spectacular volcanic plugs on earth. You may have seen it in the movie *Close Encounters of the Third Kind*.

Devil's Tower National Monument, Wyoming

What are some descriptive names for volcanoes?

El Malpais National Monument in New Mexico takes its name from Spanish words meaning "the bad country." Three million years ago, lava cracked open the ground, gushed out over a wide area, then cooled in great, jagged bumps. The terrain certainly must have looked "bad" to settlers who tried to cross it by horseback or on rickety wooden wagons.

Stromboli is known informally as "The Lighthouse of the Mediterranean" because sailors can set their course by the almost constant red glow at its summit.

Native Americans living near Mount St. Helens called the mountain Loo-Wit, "Keeper of the Fires." Or Tah-One-Lat-Clah, "Fire Mountain." Africa's highest peak is the volcanic 19,300-foot Kilimanjaro, "Demon Mountain." Mexico's Popocatepetl is Aztec for "Smoke Mountain."

Does the name "Volvo" have anything to do with "volcano"?

Nope. This Swedish car runs on gasoline, not lava fumes.

But "volcano" and related words do pop up a lot. There's Vulcano, Italy. There are towns named Volcano in Hawaii and California, and a Volcano Island in the Philippines.

The famous World War II battlefield of Iwo Jima is part of the Volcano Islands in the Pacific.

Other volcanic names: Ash, Oregon. Etna, Ohio. (And Etnas also in Indiana, Maine, New Hampshire, New York, Pennsylvania, and Wyoming!) Lava Beds, California (and Idaho and Nevada). Vesuvius, Virginia.

Do other planets have volcanoes?

Mars has plenty, including the largest ever seen. Photographs from the Mariner 9 satellite show a gigantic shield volcano called Olympus Mons. It's fifteen miles high and as wide as Ohio. Venus and Mercury also have volcanoes.

Olympus Mons volcano, Mars

What do volcanoes have in common with UFO sightings?

Nothing. But *earthquakes* just might have a connection, at least according to one controversial theory. In the 1950s, many people in New Mexico claimed to have seen glowing UFOs. A few geophysicists are now wondering whether these were really sightings of "earthquake lights." These lights are flowing, basketball-sized spheres of electricity that sometimes shoot out of the ground when earthquake stress builds up. Many of the UFO claims took place near the epicenter of three moderate-sized quakes.

Are the craters on the moon volcanic?

Most are impact-rodus from giant meteorites. But a few are volcanic. Compared to lunar impact craters twenty miles wide, lunar volcanoes are tiny and hard to see with a regular telescope. They're old too. The moon's been geologically inactive for three billion years.

Do outer space volcanoes act differently from those on earth?

Hard to say. All the extra-terrestrial volcanoes we know about look long dead, except for those on Io, one of the moons of Jupiter.

Not long ago, the Voyager 1 and 2 spacecraft photographed a beautiful orange and red volcano there. It had a mushroom-shaped plume of sulfur 175 miles high. That's far taller than any volcanic plume on earth. The reason is that Io's gravitational pull is less than ours and its atmosphere is not as dense. With seven other fiery mountains, Io is the most volcanically active place we know of in the universe other than the earth.

When will the next Mount St. Helens erupt?

On average, an eruption like the one at Mount St. Helens occurs somewhere on the planet about every ten years. A Pinatubo blows two or three times a century.

But will the world's biggest fireworks display erupt tomorrow or next week? Nobody knows for sure. We only know that it *will* eventually happen — as it has for most of the life of the earth.

What should you do if you're on a volcano and it suddenly starts rumbling?

The odds are long against this happening, but if it does — run!

Later, when you're miles away, turn around. Watch the newest land in the world boil up and explode in a fiery shower from the depths of the planet. Feel the shake, rattle, and roar of the earth changing from gas and liquid to hard rock.

This earth that we think is so solid is changing itself yet again, as it has for billions of years.

Sunset Crater Volcano National Monument, Arizona